NOTE TO PARENTS

Welcome to Kingfisher Readers! This program is designed to help young readers build skills, confidence, and a love of reading as they explore their favorite topics.

These tips can help you get more from the experience of reading books together. But remember, the most important thing is to make reading fun!

Tips to Warm Up Before Reading

- Look through the book with your child. Ask them what they notice about the pictures.
- Wonder aloud together. Ask questions and make predictions. What will this book be about? What are some words we could expect to find on these pages?

While Reading

- Take turns or read together until your child takes over.
- Point to the words as you say them.
- When your child gets stuck on a word, ask if the picture could help. Then think about the first letter too.
- Accept and praise your child's contributions.

After Reading

- Look back at the things your child found interesting. Encourage connections to other things you both know.
- Draw pictures or make models to explore these ideas.
- Read the book again soon, to build fluency.

With five distinct levels and a wealth of appealing topics, the Kingfisher Readers series provides children with an exciting way to learn to read about the world around them. Enjoy!

Ellie Costa, M.S. Ed.
Literacy Specialist, Bank Street School for Children, New York

KINGFISHER READERS

level 1

Bears

Thea Feldman

KINGFISHER
NEW YORK

KINGFISHER
LONDON & NEW YORK

Copyright © Macmillan Publishers International Ltd 2017
Published in the United States by Kingfisher,
175 Fifth Ave., New York, NY 10010
Kingfisher is an imprint of Pan Macmillan, London.
All rights reserved.

Distributed in the U.S. and Canada by Macmillan,
175 Fifth Ave., New York, NY 10010

Library of Congress Cataloging-in-Publication Data

Names: Feldman, Thea, author.
Title: Bears / Thea Feldman.
Description: New York : Kingfisher, 2017. | Series: Kingfisher readers. Level
  1 | Audience: Age 5. | Audience: Grades K to 3.
Identifiers: LCCN 2016049240| ISBN 9780753473399 (hardback) | ISBN
  9780753473405 (pbk.)
Subjects: LCSH: Bears--Juvenile literature.
Classification: LCC QL737.C27 F456 2017 | DDC 599.78--dc23
LC record available at https://lccn.loc.gov/2016049240

Series editor: Thea Feldman
Literacy consultant: Ellie Costa, Bank Street College, New York
Design: Peter Clayman

978-0-7534-7339-9 (HB)
978-0-7534-7340-5 (PB)

Kingfisher books are available for special promotions
and premiums. For details contact: Special Markets
Department, Macmillan, 175 Fifth Ave., New York, NY 10010.

For more information, please visit
www.kingfisherbooks.com

Printed in China

9 8 7 6 5 4 3 2 1

1TR/0317/WKT/UG/105MA

Picture credits
The Publisher would like to thank the following for permission to reproduce their material.
Top = t; Bottom = b; Center = c; Left = l; Right = r
Cover iStock/Marc_Latremouille; Pages 3 iStock/Dieter Meyrl; 4–5 Shutterstock/ArCaLu; 6
iStock/David Hughes; 7 iStock/Sandra vom Stein; 8 iStock/webguzs; 9 Alamy/Wayne Lynch; 10
FLPA/Imagebroker; 11 Getty/Auscape/UIG; 12 iStock/leungchopan; 13 Alamy/WILDLIFE GmbH;
14 Shutterstock/kunanon; 15 FLPA/Imagebroker; 16 Alamy/Arco Images GmbH; 17 Alamy/
Edward Parker; 18 iStock/chaney1; 19 Getty/Don Johnston; 20 Alamy/Ganesh H Shankar; 21,
22–23 FLPA/Sylvain Cordier/Biosphoto; 24 Getty/Katherine Feng; 26 Alamy/Ron Niebrugge; 27
iStock/LuCaAr; 28 iStock/Justinreznick; 29 iStock/ErikMandre; 30 Alamy/All Canada Photos; 31
iStock/Dieter Meyrl.

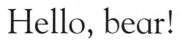

Hello, bear!

This is a brown bear.

She was asleep in a warm **den**.

She slept in the den all winter.

Now it is spring.

The brown bear comes outside.

The bear stands on her hind legs.

She sniffs the air to find food.

Brown bears eat fruit,
insects, plants, and fish.

This brown bear catches a fish
with his teeth!

There are eight kinds of bear.

The polar bear is the largest bear.

Polar bears live in the **Arctic**.

The Arctic is very cold in winter.

A polar bear hunts for seals
on the frozen ocean.

The sun bear is the smallest bear.

The sun bear lives
in a warm **forest**.

A sun bear's long tongue
can reach into **beehives**
for sweet honey!

Munch, munch, munch!

Bamboo is a panda bear's main food.

All pandas are black and white, but no two look exactly the same!

Look at the **fur** on this bear.

The pale fur on her chest
is shaped like a moon.

That is why she is called
a moon bear!

The sun bear is named
for the fur on his chest too.

Does the fur look like
the sun to you?

This is the spectacled bear.

The circles around her
eyes look like **spectacles**.

The spectacled bear is very good at climbing trees.

She builds a nest high up in the tree.

The spectacled bear eats and sleeps in the nest.

This black bear
uses her sharp
claws to climb
a tree.

Black bears look for fruit
in trees.

A sloth bear rests on
a tree branch.

Would you like to rest there?

A sloth bear has long, thick fur.

Baby sloth bears hold onto
the fur on their mother's
back to take a ride!

A baby bear is called a **cub**.

Most bears have two cubs
at the same time.

A **newborn** cub is tiny.

A baby panda weighs about 3 ounces (85 grams).

He is about the size of a stick of butter.

A panda will weigh more than 200 pounds (90 kilograms) when he grows up!

This cub is three weeks old.

Most bear cubs are born
without fur.

They cannot see or hear
when they are born.

Cubs start to see and hear when
they are about one month old.

Bear cubs stay close to their mother for the first few months of their lives.

A mother bear teaches
her cubs many things.

One day they will live
on their own.

29

Some bear cubs are born when their mother is in her den.

The cubs drink their mother's milk and grow in the den.

They stay safe there until spring.

Then they come outside for
the first time.

Hello, bear … and cub!

Glossary

Arctic the area that is the farthest north on Earth

bamboo a tall, thick, tough grass that is the main food of pandas

beehive a type of nest where bees live

cub what some baby animals, including baby bears, are called

den a safe place where some bears sleep for the winter and where some female bears give birth

forest a large piece of land that is covered with trees and other plants

fur an animal's hair

newborn an animal that has just been born

spectacles eyeglasses

If you have enjoyed reading this book, look
out for more in the Kingfisher Readers series!

KINGFISHER READERS: LEVEL 1

- [ ] Animal Colors
- [ ] Baby Animals
- [ ] Bears
- [ ] Brilliant Birds
- [ ] Busy as a Bee
- [ ] Butterflies
- [ ] Colorful Coral Reefs
- [ ] Jobs People Do
- [ ] Ladybugs
- [ ] Seals
- [ ] Seasons
- [ ] Snakes Alive!
- [ ] Tadpoles and Frogs
- [ ] Time
- [ ] Trains
- [ ] Tyrannosaurus!

**Collect
and read
them all!**

KINGFISHER READERS: LEVEL 2

- [ ] African Savanna
- [ ] Amazing Animal Senses
- [ ] Birds of Prey
- [ ] Chimpanzees
- [ ] Combine Harvesters
- [ ] Fur and Feathers
- [ ] In the Rainforest
- [ ] Sun, Moon, and Stars
- [ ] Trucks
- [ ] What Animals Eat
- [ ] What We Eat
- [ ] Where Animals Live
- [ ] Where We Live
- [ ] Your Body

For a full list of Kingfisher Readers books, plus guidance for
teachers and parents and activities and fun stuff for kids, go to
the Kingfisher Readers website: www.kingfisherreaders.com